MAXnotes®

John Steinbeck's

Of Mice and Men

Text by

Joseph E. Scalia
(M.A., Brooklyn College)
Department of English
Hicksville High School
Hicksville, New York

Lena T. Shamblin
(M.A., Mississippi State University)
Department of English
West Bolivar District High School
Rosedale, Mississippi

Illustrations by
Karen Pica

Research & Education Association
Visit our website at
www.rea.com

Research & Education Association
61 Ethel Road West
Piscataway, New Jersey 08854
E-mail: info@rea.com

MAXnotes® for
OF MICE AND MEN

Year 2008 Printing

Printed in the United States of America

Library of Congress Control Number 00-191838

International Standard Book Number 0-87891-997-X

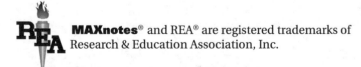

MAXnotes® and REA® are registered trademarks of
Research & Education Association, Inc.

What **MAXnotes** *Will Do for You*

This book is intended to help you absorb the essential contents and features of John Steinbeck's *Of Mice and Men* and to help you gain a thorough understanding of the work. Our book has been designed to do this more quickly and effectively than any other study guide.

For best results, this **MAXnotes** book should be used as a companion to the actual work, not instead of it. The interaction between the two will greatly benefit you.

To help you in your studies, this book presents the most up-to-date interpretations of every section of the actual work, followed by questions and fully explained answers that will enable you to analyze the material critically. The questions also will help you to test your understanding of the work and will prepare you for discussions and exams.

Meaningful illustrations are included to further enhance your understanding and enjoyment of the literary work. The illustrations are designed to place you into the mood and spirit of the work's settings.

This **MAXnotes** book analyzes and summarizes each section as you go along, with discussions of the characters and explanations of the plot. A biography of the author and examination of the work's historical context will help you put this literary piece into the proper framework of what is taking place.

The use of this study guide will save you the hours of preparation time that would ordinarily be required to arrive at a complete grasp of this work of literature. You will be well prepared for classroom discussions, homework, and exams. The guidelines that are included for writing papers and reports on various topics will prepare you for any added work that may be assigned.

The **MAXnotes** will take your grades "to the max."

Larry B. Kling
Chief Editor

Contents

> **Each chapter includes List of Characters,
> Summary, Analysis, Study Questions and
> Answers, and Suggested Essay Topics.**

MAXnotes® are simply the best – but don't just take our word for it...

"... I have told every bookstore in the area to carry your MAXnotes. They are the only notes I recommend to my students. There is no comparison between MAXnotes and all other notes ..."
 – *High School Teacher & Reading Specialist,*
 Arlington High School, Arlington, MA

"... I discovered the MAXnotes when a friend loaned me her copy of the *MAXnotes for Romeo and Juliet.* The book really helped me understand the story. Please send me a list of stores in my area that carry the MAXnotes. I would like to use more of them ..."
 – *Student, San Marino, CA*

"... The two MAXnotes titles that I have used have been very, very useful in helping me understand the subject matter reviewed. Thank you for creating the MAXnotes series ..."
 – *Student, Morrisville, PA*

A Glance at Some of the Characters

George Milton

Lennie Small

Slim

Candy

Crooks

Whit

Curley

Curley's Wife

SECTION ONE

Introduction

The Life and Work of John Steinbeck

Born February 27, 1902, in Salinas, California, not far from the setting of his novel *Of Mice and Men*, John Steinbeck was the grandson of a German immigrant on his father's side (whose name was originally Grossteinbeck), and of an Irish immigrant on his mother's side. Both his father and his grandfather had been independent businessmen who owned and operated their own flour mill. His father also served as county treasurer for 11 years before retiring. Steinbeck's mother was the daughter of a California rancher. She was a schoolteacher.

As educated people of some affluence, Steinbeck's parents offered their children a variety of cultural experiences. The family regularly attended plays and concerts. Listening to their parents read was a customary after-dinner ritual for the Steinbeck children. Books were often prized holiday gifts.

From boyhood, John Steinbeck dreamed of being a writer. This youthful aspiration was not simply a dream, though. It was the goal that shaped his life. Even as a boy he spent part of each day writing. While the rest of the neighborhood slept, he sat in his room working for hours on short stories, which he submitted only anonymously. His early material was often rejected, but he remained undaunted.

After making "B's" through high school, Steinbeck entered Stanford University. He attended college there for five years, but he never completed requirements for graduation. Constantly working on his fiction, Steinbeck took several college writing courses and published a few pieces in Stanford's literary journals, but when he submitted his creative works to magazines, he still received only rejections. He left Stanford at the age of 23 and moved to New York, hoping to become a writer. He got a job as a reporter but was ultimately dismissed since he was, admittedly, not very good at it. Somewhat discouraged, Steinbeck returned to California where he took on various odd jobs, all the while continuing to work on his fiction.

Following Steinbeck's 1930 marriage to Carol Henning, he experienced his most successful decade. During their marriage, which lasted for a little over 10 years, Steinbeck came into his own as a writer and produced some of his best fiction. One reason was that early in the marriage, Carol allowed him to focus exclusively on his art. While he remained home writing, she worked to support them both.

Although he was writing diligently, Steinbeck won neither financial success nor critical acclaim with his early novels: *Cup of Gold* (1929), *The Pastures of Heaven* (1932), and *To a God Unknown* (1933). But all of this changed with the publication of *Tortilla Flat* (1935), which brought him immediate fame and wealth. This was to be the first of his bestsellers. The following year *In Dubious Battle* (1936) was published. Success, financial and critical, followed with the publication of *Of Mice and Men* (1937). The novel was produced on Broadway later that same year, and it won the Drama Critics' Circle Award. *The Grapes of Wrath* (1939) won Steinbeck the Pulitzer Prize for fiction and a place in the National Institute of Arts and Letters.

But Steinbeck did not confine himself to the arena of fiction. Already practiced in publishing articles for newspapers, he wrote his first non-fiction book—*Sea of Cortez* (1941)—with his longtime friend Ed Ricketts. The book is based on the time Steinbeck spent with Ricketts on the Gulf of California collecting marine specimens.

With the beginning of a new decade came several endings for Steinbeck. In the late 1930s came the deterioration of Steinbeck's marriage to Carol. In 1942, Carol divorced him. The next year he married Gwyndolen Conger Verdon and moved to New York. While this five-year marriage did give him his only two children, Tom and John, it marks the point at which the quality of his fiction began its decline.

Following his second marriage, and the move from his native California, Steinbeck published nearly a dozen novels. Though each of these show merit, on the whole, none match the excellence of his works of the 1930s. He continued, however, to follow the "drive" he had identified in a letter to his publisher: "making people understand each other."

The Moon Is Down (1942), like *Of Mice and Men*, was written as a novel-play. As with *Of Mice and Men*, it was intended to illuminate a facet of the world Steinbeck's audience did not understand. The novel focused on World War II and the Nazi occupation of Scandinavia.

As his personal contribution to the war cause, Steinbeck wrote *Bombs Away* (1942) for the Army Air Corps. Steinbeck's wartime efforts were highly successful. The book was successful in helping to recruit soldiers, and royalties from the movie were contributed to the Air Corps. Later, for six months in 1943, Steinbeck took a more active role in the war, and served as the New York *Herald Tribune* war correspondent in the European war zone.

Cannery Row (1945) depicts a group of men who, instead of being displaced by society, have deliberately detached themselves from the social system. It is set in the pre-war 1930s and reflects his continued concern with social deviants.

The Pearl (1947) appeared first as a motion picture script. Steinbeck though, was reportedly not eager to continue in this medium. *The Pearl* was subsequently revised into a long magazine story and then a book. Steinbeck has called this his "folk tale" and likens it to a parable. The plot of this short novel is loosely based on a true story Steinbeck heard while he was in Mexico working on his *Sea of Cortez*. An account published in *Sea of Cortez* describes a young Indian's discovery of "the Pearl of the World." Ironically his good fortune, an assurance of physical and religious security, only brings him misery, and the story ends with the young Indian throwing the cursed pearl back into the sea.

Two of Steinbeck's final novels—*East of Eden* (1952) and *The Winter of Our Discontent* (1961)—mark a return to the past. *East of Eden* returns to his familiar California setting as he portrays the fictional account of his mother's family. *The Winter of Our Discontent* focuses on the superiority of things of the past.

During the 1950s, Steinbeck continued to express his social and political views, but in a new way. He helped write speeches for the 1952 and 1956 presidential campaigns. He even served as advisor to President Johnson. For his advisory services during the years of the Vietnam conflict, Steinbeck was awarded the United States Medal of Freedom in 1964.

Continuing to experiment with narrative forms, Steinbeck published several non-fiction forms late in his career. A *Russian Journal* (1948) is an account of his travels in Russia. *Travels with Charley* (1962) records his thoughts while traveling the country with his dog, Charley. He also published *The Log*

from the Sea of Cortez (1951) which included a biographical
sketch of Ricketts, his valued friend who had died a few years
earlier. *Once There Was a War* (1958) was his publication of
wartime dispatches.

Though Steinbeck never again recaptured the glory of
the 1930s, his stature as one of America's foremost novelists
remained. In 1948 he was elected to the American Academy
of Letters. In 1962 he was awarded the Nobel Prize for literature. He had won his place in American literary history.

He had also found happiness in marriage. Steinbeck
married Elaine Scott in 1950. They were together, happily
according to Steinbeck, until his death in late 1968.

Historical Background

Steinbeck drew heavily from his own experiences. Four
of his novels, *Tortilla Flat, Of Mice and Men, In Dubious
Battle,* and *The Grapes of Wrath,* and several short stories
are set in and around his hometown of Salinas, California.
Reflecting his own love of central California, these stories take
place in towns, ranches, and valleys that lie between the
Gabilan Mountains and the coastal Santa Lucia Mountains.

Steinbeck was also acutely aware of the social and economic problems of the times. Having lived during the Great
Depression of the 1930s, during bread lines and soup kitch-
ens, during labor unrest and escalating unemployment, he
was spared the suffering that befell so many. But he knew
first hand the problems that they faced.

Before the Great Depression, and between sessions at
Stanford University, Steinbeck worked at odd jobs on California ranches. During one summer early in his college career, Steinbeck bucked barley on a ranch just south of Salinas.
These experiences exposed him to the lower strata of society and provided him with material that would later appear
in his novels of the 1930s.

Tortilla Flat (1935) drew on his experiences with California migrant workers living on the outer fringes of society. This was his first attempt to rouse an audience's pity for the conditions of transient laborers, but it was not to be his last. Steinbeck continued to speak for the exploited man with *In Dubious Battle* (1936). This controversial novel was an account of migrant workers caught in a California labor strike. Steinbeck had witnessed up close the intolerable conditions under which these men were forced to work. He had seen certain groups who were badly hurt by the system in which they lived. In the novel he tried to create something meaningful from the behavior of these exploited people who were not able to speak for themselves.

Of Mice and Men (1937) maintains this focus on the migrant worker, here portraying his elusive dream of owning his own land. This is the same dream shared and lost by so many of the Depression era.

Following *Of Mice and Men*, Steinbeck continued his research into migrant worker conditions by spending four weeks with them, sharing in their living and working routines. He published several feature articles that reported on the dismal conditions he found. Steinbeck also drew from this experience while writing his Pulitzer Prize-winning *The Grapes of Wrath* (1939).

Master List of Characters

George Milton—*The migrant ranch hand who takes care of Lennie. He is one of two main protagonists in the story. He is slender, small and quick, with a dark face, restless eyes, and sharp features. Taking care of Lennie shows George's need for companionship, but also his high moral character and compassion because Lennie is such a burden and George is completely loyal to him. George dreams of owning a small farm of his own, but his dream is lost.*

Lennie Small—*George's mildly retarded travelling companion and the other main protagonist in the story. He is a huge man, with large, pale eyes, a shapeless face, and sloping shoulders. Lennie is frequently portrayed in animal terms and loves to pet soft things. His name is an example of irony because he is large and possesses incredible physical strength, yet he has the mind of a child. Lennie also dreams of owning a farm with his friend George, but Lennie causes the ruin of their dream.*

Slim—*The master "skinner" or mule driver of the ranch. He is tall man with long black hair who does not feel the need to wear high-heeled boots. Respected by all, Slim is a master at his trade and has moral authority over the other men. Quiet, grave, and perceptive, he invites confidence by accepting people as they are. Slim respects Lennie's hard work and consoles George when Lennie dies.*

Candy—*The old crippled ranch hand who has lost a hand. Afraid of being fired when he gets too old to work, he offers his life savings to become a part of George and Lennie's dream. His companion is an equally old crippled dog that stinks; after Candy allows Carlson to kill the dog, he regrets not having done it himself.*

Crooks—*The black stable hand who is proud and aloof. His spine has been left crooked from a horse's kick, and he rubs liniment on his painful back. Bitter and lonely, Crooks lives in isolation in the harness room. His only recreations are an occasional game of horseshoes with other men, but most of the time he spends by himself reading. He listens with longing to Lennie tell of his dream ranch and he yearns to be part of it.*

Carlson—*The big-bellied ranch worker who kills Candy's old dog. Practical and down to earth, he focuses on actions*

*and doesn't notice people's feelings. He provides the gun
used by George to kill Lennie.*

Curley—*The boss's son. A little man, he is always looking for
a fight, especially with men who are bigger than he. Curley
has brown face and eyes, tightly curled hair, and a hot
temper, and prides himself on having been a welterweight
boxer. Recently married, he spends much of his time looking for his pretty wife.*

Curley's wife—*The pretty, flirtatious, and unnamed wife of
Curley. She has red lips and fingernails and wears heavy
makeup. Her hair hangs in tight sausage curls, and her
red shoes are decorated at the instep with red ostrich feathers. She is said by the men to give them "the eye," and they
brand her as a "tramp." She knows Curley is mean and
does not like him. In her loneliness and unhappiness, she
tries to make friends with Lennie. She is never given a
name in the story.*

The boss—*Another unnamed character. He is a short, stocky
man wearing high-heeled boots with spurs to show that
he is not a laborer. Like his son, the boss has a hot temper
and frequently takes his anger out on Crooks. At Christmas, he brought in a gallon of whiskey for the boys in the
bunk house. He is suspicious of George's interest in Lennie.*

Whit—*A young laboring man on the ranch. He is friendly and
likes to talk, but he is already stooped from the hard work
on the ranch. He reads a letter to the editor of a Western
magazine written by a former worker at the ranch.*

Summary of the Novel

Before reporting for work, migrant workers George
Milton and Lennie Small spend the night on a peaceful
riverbank. For the second time, George has to take away a

dead mouse that Lennie has been petting. He consoles Lennie by recounting the story of their dream farm where Lennie will tend rabbits.

Before retiring, George tells Lennie to remember this place by the river, because if Lennie ever gets into trouble he must return here and hide in the brush until George comes for him.

Friday, in the ranch's bunkhouse, the men meet Candy, the old, crippled swamper; the boss's arrogant son, Curley, who is always ready to fight; and Curley's new wife, who is pretty and flirtatious.

Also entering the bunkhouse are Slim, an experienced and respected work-team leader, and Carlson, a ranch hand. Both men are friendly and welcome George and Lennie to the ranch.

Friday night, after a half day's work, Lennie goes to the barn to visit the puppy Slim has given him. Back in the bunkhouse, George confesses to a sympathetic Slim that they left their previous job because Lennie was accused of attacking a girl.

Later that evening, when Candy's dog, lame and blind with age, enters the bunkhouse, Carlson suggests that Candy shoot it to put it out of its misery. Candy reluctantly agrees to allow Carlson to shoot the dog with his Luger pistol. Though deeply saddened at the death of his longtime companion, Candy says later that he should have shot his dog himself, instead of letting a stranger do it.

Sitting in the bunkhouse, George and Lennie again talk of their dream farm. Listening quietly, old Candy offers his life's savings, half of the money they will need to buy the farm, if he can become a partner in their dream.

Curley and Slim return to the bunkhouse, arguing about Curley's wife. Curley sees Lennie smiling and accuses Lennie of laughing at him. He punches Lennie without retaliation. When George finally gives the word, though, Lennie catches Curley's hand and crushes it.

Saturday night, while the others are in town, Lennie wanders into Crooks's room, where Crooks tells Lennie of his loneliness. After Candy joins them, Curley's wife comes in. When they try to get her to leave, she professes her own loneliness and makes a deliberate attempt to talk to Lennie, but she is driven away by the return of the other ranch hands.

The next day, Sunday, Lennie returns to the barn to pet his puppy. Curley's wife comes in, talks to Lennie, and lets him caress her hair. When she tries to make him stop, he panics and accidentally breaks her neck. Realizing she is dead, Lennie flees.

Candy and George discover the body of Curley's wife, and they know the other men will want Lennie lynched. As the men are preparing a search party, Carlson announces that his gun is missing. In spite of George's insistence that Lennie would never kill on purpose, the men want Lennie shot on sight.

At the riverbank awaiting George, Lennie is confronted with images of his dead aunt and a giant rabbit, both chastising him for disappointing George. When George arrives, he comforts his friend. As he hears the others nearing, he helps Lennie imagine, for the last time, their dream farm. With great difficulty, he places Carlson's revolver at the back of Lennie's head and pulls the trigger.

Only Slim understands what has happened. He comforts George and reassures him that this was what he had to do.

Estimated Reading Time

Of Mice and Men is one of Steinbeck's short novels. It is only six chapters long, and about one hundred pages. It reads rather quickly, and it should take the average reader fewer than four hours to complete.

The novel can be divided into four sections, corresponding to the four days entailed in the plot, with each section taking place on a different day. Chapter 1 takes place on the Thursday night the men spend by the river. Chapters 2 and 3 cover Friday. Chapter 4 occurs on Saturday night. Chapters 5 and 6 contain the events of Sunday.

SECTION TWO

Chapter 1

New Characters:

George Milton: *migrant worker who cares for Lennie Small*

Lennie Small: *mildly retarded migrant worker, George's companion*

Summary

Following a worn path from the highway, George Milton and Lennie Small come upon the peaceful banks of the Salinas River and stop to rest. After drinking from the river, George reminds Lennie of their destination, a ranch just up the highway where they will work bucking barley.

Sitting in this haven along the banks of the river, George notices Lennie has something in his pocket. When he makes Lennie give it to him, he discovers it is a dead mouse. Lennie says he has been petting it as they walked along. George throws the dead mouse away.

In the evening, George sends Lennie to collect firewood and hears him splash in the water. When he returns, George demands that Lennie hand over the dead mouse. Lennie had retrieved it from the brush pile where George had thrown it.

When Lennie begins to cry, George promises him a fresh mouse. In his frustration, he openly laments being burdened with the responsibility of Lennie. When Lennie offers to go

off by himself, George recants and says they have to stick together. Together they have someone to care about them and they have a future, a dream of owning their own farm with rabbits that Lennie will tend.

Before retiring George asks Lennie to try to remember what this place looks like. If Lennie gets into trouble at the new job, he is to hide here in the brush until George comes for him.

Recalling their dream, they drift to sleep on the banks of the river beside the dying fire.

Analysis

Setting is the physical location for the story, as well as the general time frame when it takes place. It includes the specific duration of time it takes the author to unfold his plot. Most of *Of Mice and Men* takes place on and about a ranch in the Salinas Valley, near the town of Soledad, south of San Francisco. The story begins and ends at a clearing near a pool about a quarter of a mile from the ranch, and spans only four days. Although the book was published in 1937, Steinbeck does not allude to the Depression in the novel. His characters are engaged in their smaller, private economic struggles, giving the work a sense of timelessness and universality.

Point of view refers to the vantage point from which the story is told. It is the "eyes" through which the reader sees the unfolded events, the "voice" used by the narrator to tell the tale. In *Of Mice and Men*, Steinbeck uses the omniscient or all-knowing point of view. He gets into the minds of his characters, revealing their inner thoughts, and he describes things that the characters themselves do not know. This omniscient point of view allows the reader a broader insight into people and events. In the opening chapter, Steinbeck describes the clearing by the pool before the arrival of George and Lennie.

The setting of the opening chapter is described in lyrical detail by Steinbeck. A few miles south of Soledad ("loneliness"), the river "runs deep and green" and the water is "warm too, for it has slipped twinkling over the yellow sands in the sunlight." On the valley side of the Gabilan mountains, the water is lined with graceful sycamores and willows. Lizards, 'coons, dogs, and deer come to the pool, and there is a path beaten by boys come to swim and tramps come to rest. This is a place of peace, a refuge from heat and work. To this green pool come George and Lennie, and Steinbeck has his two main characters enter in single file. Although both are dressed in nondescript denim clothes of working men, the one takes charge and the other follows. George is small, quick, nervous, and sharp. Lennie, who walks behind George even in the open, is large, shapeless, and strong. Lennie flops down and begins to gulp water, prompting George to shake his companion lest he drink too much and "get sick like you was last night." To Lennie's simple mind, the water is good and he does not worry if it "looks kinda scummy" and isn't running. George's concern for Lennie is apparent from the first scene, and so is Lennie's adoration of his friend. Lennie even tries to sit embracing his knees with his arms, just like George, looks over to see if the posture is just right, and then "pulled his hat down a little more over his eyes, the way George's hat was."

George has chosen to spend the night by this pool instead of hike the remaining distance to the ranch. Tired from walking because the bus driver had let them out too early, George and Lennie need rest before they begin the heavy work of bucking grain bags. As dusk comes on, nature settles peacefully to rest. A big carp comes to the surface of the pool and disappears, tufts of willow cotton settle on the water, and sycamore leaves rustle in the night breeze. At the end of the first chapter, George and Lennie have settled to sleep by

the fire, which is burning down comfortably to coals. George and Lennie are represented as part of nature here. The sound of a coyote and a responding dog serve to show the two men as comfortable with all of nature, and their stay here is much more peaceful than any foray into life among men. In an essay for the *Saturday Review*, Steinbeck writes, "I believe that man is a double thing—a group animal and at the same time an individual. And it occurs to me that he cannot successfully be the second until he has fulfilled the first." George and Lennie always have difficulty with the first—Lennie because of his simple mind and great strength, and George because he chooses to care for Lennie. Throughout the novel, Steinbeck associates Lennie with animal movements, and Lennie's love of dogs and rabbits brings about the tragedy of the novel.

In the description he first mentions the rabbits, which will become a significant symbol throughout the book. Their softness is Lennie's soft heart. They represent independence and freedom. They are symbolic of everything George and Lennie hope to attain, their piece of land and their peace of mind.

> On the sand banks the rabbits sat as quietly as little gray sculptured stones. And then from the direction of the state highway came the sound of footsteps on crisp sycamore leaves. The rabbits hurried noiselessly for cover. A stilted heron labored up into the air and pounded down river. For a moment the place was lifeless, and then two men emerged from the path and came into the opening by the green pool.

Steinbeck has structured this novel much like a play. The first chapter, and each succeeding section begins with a setting of the scene. Virtually all of the novel consists of dialogue, through which the characters provide an explanation of themselves, rather than being explained by the narrator. The narrator rarely intrudes into the work, except to specify a character's words or actions, similar to the stage directions in a play.

In this first chapter Steinbeck introduces one of the major themes of the novel, the theme of loneliness. It is part of the itinerant workers' lives and it is the primary reason Lennie and George are together. This is expressed in the opening dialogue. Angry at Lennie because he wants ketchup with his beans, George erupts.

> "Whatever we ain't got, that's what you want. God a'mighty, if I was alone I could live so easy. I could go get a job an' work, an' no trouble. No mess at all, and when the end of the month come I could take my fifty bucks and go into town and get whatever I want... An' whatta I got," George went on furiously. "I got you!"

Lennie's threat, one he has apparently made before, to run off to a cave and leave George alone, a place where he can find a mouse and keep it, is enough to stop George's protests. Their little flare up ends with George's affirmation of their bond and friendship.

> "Guys like us, that work on ranches, are the loneliest guys in the world.... They ain't got nothing to look ahead to...."

Lennie broke in. *"But not us! An' why?*
Because....because I got you to look after me, and
you got me to look after you, and that's why."

Steinbeck establishes the ironic relationship between
George Milton and Lennie Small. George, a small man with
sharp features, is the mental and physical opposite of his
companion. Lennie is a huge man with a child's mind. The
basic conflict, as drawn out in Chapter 1, is not so much
between George and Lennie, as it is between these two men
and the rest of the world. They fight to keep alive their dream
of independence in a world that defeats dreams and leaves
men like themselves caught in a hopeless cycle of working
and spending, working and spending.

The animal imagery used to describe George character-
izes him as a pet. He drinks from the pool "like a horse" and
he scoops up water with his "paw." When George demands
the mouse Lennie is hiding, Lennie hands it over "like a
terrier...to its master." Lennie is, in several respects, like
George's pet. He entertains George and keeps him company
in the lonely life of the migrant worker.

Throughout the novel Lennie is associated with rabbits.
When the men first come upon the river, rabbits scurry into
the underbrush. Lennie speaks often of tending to the rabbits on the farm he and George dream of buying. And in the
final chapter, which takes place in the same setting as the
first chapter, he is approached by an imaginary man-sized
talking rabbit.

But Lennie is more than a pet. He is what gives purpose
to George's life. As George explains to Lennie, only together
can they have somebody to care about them, somewhere to
belong, a future. Having each other is all that separates them
from the other migrant workers who are the loneliest people
in the world.

Because they have a relationship based on genuine affection, Lennie is willing to tolerate George's abuses and George is willing to suffer the frustrations and inconveniences of taking care of a childlike Lennie.

One such frustration is the situation they have just fled. They have had to run away from Weed, the last place they were working, because Lennie wanted to pet a girl's pretty dress, and scared her. While this underscores his innocent love of things that are pretty and soft, it also foreshadows the eventual death of Curley's wife. She, too, becomes Lennie's unintentional victim because she is pretty and has soft hair that he wants to pet.

Death plays an important role in the story, and Steinbeck introduces it when he describes the dead mouse carried by Lennie. Events of the following days are foreshadowed by George's words to the blubbering Lennie: "That mouse ain't fresh, Lennie; and besides, you've broke it pettin' it." Steinbeck establishes Lennie's ability to kill simply because he is unable to control his own strength. Another example of foreshadowing is found in George's reference to Weed, the town they had to flee because of an incident involving a young woman.

> "Jus' wanted to feel that girl's dress— jus' wanted to pet it like it was a mouse — Well, how the hell did she know you jus' wanted to feel her dress? She jerks back and you hold on like it was a mouse. She yells and we got to hide in a irrigation ditch all day with guys lookin' for us, and we got to sneak out in the dark and get outta the country. All the time somethin' like that—all the time."

It is interesting to note Steinbeck's dual style in the work. He alternates between a poetic and a naturalistic style. The

dialogue, which makes up the bulk of the novel, is written in dialect, slang, and colloquialisms. It is intentionally ungrammatical and natural. But Steinbeck's descriptions of the settings at the beginning of each chapter are flowing, lyrical and poetic.

It is worth mentioning here that Steinbeck's title, *Of Mice and Men*, comes from a poem, "To a Mouse," published in 1785 by the Scottish poet Robert Burns. It contains the lines, "The best laid schemes o' mice an' men/ Gang aft a gley." Translated as, "The best laid plans of mice and men often go astray," it reflects the theme of the novel, the loss of a dream. George and Lennie's hopes for the American Dream, "to live off the fatta the lan'", will be crushed as easily as the mouse.

Study Questions

1. When George and Lennie approach the river, why does George warn Lennie not to drink too much water?

2. What has George told Lennie about that he always remembers even when he forgets everything else?

3. Why does Lennie have a dead mouse in his pocket?

4. Why does George order Lennie not to talk when they get to the ranch?

5. What happened to all of the mice that Lennie's Aunt Clara gave him?

6. Why have George and Lennie run away from Weed?

7. What does Lennie want to eat with his beans?

8. Why does George say that migrant workers who travel from farm to farm are the loneliest people in the world?

9. What dream do George and Lennie share?

10. What does George tell Lennie to do if he gets in trouble at their new job site?

Of Mice and Men

Answers

1. George says Lennie will be sick like he was the night before.

2. Lennie always remembers that he will be the one to tend the rabbits on their dream farm.

3. He is carrying it in his pocket so he can pet it as they walk. He likes to pet soft things.

4. George says that if the boss hears Lennie talk before he sees Lennie work, the two men won't have a chance of getting the job.

5. He killed the mice by petting them too hard.

6. Lennie tried to feel a girl's dress. He wanted to pet the dress but she thought he was attacking her.

7. Lennie wants ketchup to put on his beans.

8. He says migrant workers are lonely because they don't have any family, they don't belong anywhere, and they have nothing to look forward to.

9. They share the dream of buying a small farm together and working it. On this farm Lennie will tend the rabbits and pet them whenever he wants.

10. George tells Lennie to come to this spot where they are camping and hide in the bushes until George comes for him.

Suggested Essay Topics

1. George and Lennie are obviously committed to each other, yet they often criticize each other or threaten to leave. Examine the negative aspects of this relationship, and then consider why they stay together in spite of all of this. Contrast the language of each, their threats and complaints, with what they really feel. What is it that so strongly binds these two together?

2. Write a character profile of Lennie and George. In addition to describing their physical characteristics, focus on their personalities, their hopes, and their dreams. How is each character different, and how do they complement each other?

Chapter 2

New Characters:

Candy: *the one-handed ranch custodian*

The Boss: *runs the barley farm*

Curley: *the boss's newly married, hot-headed son*

Curley's wife: *the pretty, flirtatious, unnamed wife of Curley*

Slim: *a jerkline skinner, the respected authority on the ranch*

Carlson: *an experienced ranch hand*

Summary

Chapter 2 takes place in the bunkhouse of the barley ranch on Friday morning. George and Lennie enter the bunkhouse behind Candy, the old crippled swamper, an unskilled laborer who cleans up the bunkhouse. He shows them to their two beds and tells George and Lennie about the ranch, about the boss, and about Crooks, the stable buck. When George sees a can of bug killer left by the man who last occupied the bed, a blacksmith, he is concerned about lice. Candy reassures him that the place is clean, and that the boss is a fair man.

After George and Lennie finish making their beds, the boss comes in. When he questions the men about reporting

late for work, he notices that George always answers for Lennie. Upon hearing Lennie talk, the man realizes Lennie's mental state. It makes him suspicious and he interrogates George. He asks George if he is traveling with Lennie just to take advantage of his traveling companion. But George allays his suspicions, at least for the time, and he lies to the boss, saying that Lennie is his cousin who was kicked in the head by a horse when he was younger. When the boss leaves, George scolds Lennie for talking because now the boss is watching them. George tells Lennie to keep his mouth shut and let George do all of the talking.

Shortly after the boss leaves, Candy reappears. George accuses Candy, who was sweeping up the bunkhouse, of listening in on their conversation. Candy says, "I didn't hear nothing you guys was sayin'. I ain't interested in nothing you was sayin'. A guy on a ranch don't never listen nor he don't ast no questions." And then their attentions turn to Candy's old, lame dog.

Candy is followed by the boss's son, Curley, who barges into the bunkhouse. When Curley sees the size of Lennie, he automatically goes into a boxer's stance and insists that Lennie talk to him. But when his attempts to pick a fight with Lennie fail, he leaves the bunkhouse.

Candy tells the two new workers that Curley was a boxer and that he tries to pick fights with every man he meets, especially men who are bigger than he. Since Curley is the boss's son, he is in no danger of getting fired. Candy also tells them about Curley's new wife of two weeks, who has started hanging around the bunkhouse and flirting with most of the ranch hands.

After Candy leaves, the two of them discuss Curley. George explains to Lennie how Curley is the type who is always looking for trouble. His advice to Lennie is to keep away from him. Lennie is afraid that Curley will hurt him, and

George tells him to keep his mouth shut and go to the other side of the room whenever Curley is around. "Don't let him pull you in," he advises his friend, "—but—if the son-of-a-bitch socks you—let 'im have it." Then he reminds Lennie of their arrangement if Lennie ever gets into trouble. George tells him that he is to go hide in the brush down by the river where they had camped the night before and wait there until George arrives.

Again their conversation is interrupted when they realize someone has come into the room. It is Curley's young wife who enters the bunkhouse looking for her husband. Though her visit is brief, it is enough for Lennie to decide she is beautiful and for George to decide that she is a troublesome tramp.

When Slim, the ranch authority and sage, comes into the bunkhouse, he interviews the new men as did the boss and his son, but with a gentle and friendly manner. He also introduces them to Carlson, a powerful, big-stomached ranch hand. Carlson asks Slim about his dog and her puppies and suggests giving Candy one to replace his smelly, old dog. Anticipating Lennie's request, George agrees to ask Slim if Lennie can also have one of the puppies, a brown and white one.

The chapter ends when Curley comes back into the bunkhouse looking for trouble and also for his wife. "Ya know, Lennie," George tells him, "I'm scared I'm gonna tangle with that bastard myself. I hate his guts. Jesus Christ!"

Analysis

In this chapter Steinbeck introduces his audience to the other characters on the ranch, painting a picture of bunkhouse life for the migrant workers of the 1930s. The space needed for their personal belongings was minimal. They accumulated few possessions, for they knew that their stay

in one place was only temporary and whatever they owned would have to be carried with them on their backs.

This is evident in the scene at the beginning of the chapter, when George and Lennie enter the bunkhouse. The other ranch hands have already gone out into the fields, allowing them an opportunity to settle in before going out for the afternoon. While they are inspecting their bunks, George finds a can of bug killer that belonged to the man who formerly occupied the bed. George is concerned about lice, which he calls "pants rabbits" or "graybacks." It is only one example of Steinbeck's use of realistic slang words and colloquialisms. Candy describes Whitey, the last man that had the bed, as a "hell of a nice fella and as clean a guy as you want to meet. Used to wash his hands even *after* he ate." Whitey was the kind of guy who used to peel his boiled potatoes and take out every spot. And if there was a red splotch on an egg, he'd scrape it off. He'd dress up on Sundays and put on a necktie just to sit around the bunkhouse.

According to Candy's assessment, Whitey was so clean and so concerned about conditions on the ranch that he quit. "Why....he....just quit, the way a guy will. Says it was the food. Just wanted to move. Didn't give no other reason but the food. Just says 'gimme my time' one night, the way any guy would."

The boss's suspicion that George is taking advantage of Lennie emphasizes the tendency of the ranch man to avoid forming connections. When George continually speaks for Lennie and then when Lennie speaks for himself, revealing his mental condition, the boss feels certain that George is using Lennie. He asks if George is taking Lennie's pay from him, because in this walk of life a ranch man doesn't "take so much trouble for another guy." Even after George makes an excuse, saying that Lennie is his cousin who's been kicked in the head by a horse, the boss remains suspicious and promises to keep an eye on him. Note the economical way in which Steinbeck describes the man.

> He wore blue jean trousers, a flannel shirt, a black, unbuttoned vest and a black coat. His thumbs were stuck in his belt, on each side of a square steel buckle. On his head was a soiled brown Stetson hat, and he wore high-heeled boots and spurs to prove he was not a laboring man.

Curley, the boss's son, recognizes something special about Lennie too, but he views him as his potential adversary instead of as a potential victim for George. As soon as he sees Lennie, he goes into a fighter's stance. The boss's son, like his father, tries to make Lennie talk. When George intervenes, Curley parrots his father's question, asking George why he's getting involved, and equally suspicious when he hears that they travel together. Steinbeck describes him as a thin young man with a brown face, with brown eyes, and a head of "tightly curled hair." Like his father, he wears high-heeled boots, which are more for show and unnecessary on a grain farm, according to Candy. He also wears a work glove on his left hand, which, Candy tells George, is "fulla vaseline" to keep his hand soft for his young wife.

Both the boss and Curley wear high-heeled boots to show they are above the others. Candy, the old swamper, tells George and Lennie that the boss has a temper and vents his anger on the black stable buck. Candy also explains that when Curley jumps a big guy and beats him, everyone says what a "game guy" Curley is; but if the big guy wins, then people say the big guy should have picked on someone his own size. It seems Curley never gives anyone a fair chance, but he doesn't care because he is the boss's son and will never be fired. The glove Curley wears, therefore, becomes a symbol of his pugnacious, vicious nature, as well as his desire to control his new wife.

Steinbeck's description of Slim is the most detailed. He is tall with long black hair. He moves with "a majesty only achieved by royalty and master craftsmen." A jerkline skinner, he is capable of driving twenty mules with a single line, of "killing a fly on the wheeler's butt with a bull whip without touching the mule." According to Candy, "Slim don't need to wear no high-heeled boots on a grain team." There is a "gravity in his manner and a quiet so profound that all talk stopped when he spoke." He is ageless, thirty-five or fifty. "His ear heard more than was said to him, and his slow speech had overtones not of thought, but of understanding beyond thought." Slim is bigger than life, the "prince of the ranch" whose "authority was so great that his word was taken on any subject." Gentle and kind, he expresses no surprise that George and Lennie travel together. Instead Slim muses over why more men don't. He concludes, "Maybe ever'body in the whole damn world is scared of each other."

Finally there is Curley's wife. She has full rouged lips, wide-spaced eyes, and heavy makeup. Her fingernails are red and her hair "hung in little rolled clusters, like sausages." She is never given a name by Steinbeck, and throughout the book she is referred to as Curley's wife. She is depicted not as a complete human being, but as an unwelcomed annoyance, a nuisance, and an obstacle to the legitimate work on the ranch. The men regard her as dangerous. Candy calls her a "tart." And George sees her as a threat, especially to Lennie who is fond of soft things. After his brief meeting with her, George tells Lennie, "Don't you even take a look at that bitch.... I seen 'em poison before, but I never seen no piece of jail bait worse than her. You leave her be." It will turn out to be good advice.

At first Lennie is almost hypnotized by Curley's wife as she appears in the doorway wearing her cotton house dress and red mules with bouquets of red ostrich feathers on the insteps. Fascinated, Lennie watches as she puts her hands behind her body and arches it seductively forward. No one except Slim is comfortable with her. As he enters the bunkhouse, he casually calls to her "Hi, Good-lookin'." When she says she is looking for Curley, Slim jokes that she must not be looking very hard because Curley just entered their house. She becomes "suddenly apprehensive" and hurries away, evidently afraid of her new husband.

When Lennie says twice that he thinks Curley's wife is "purty," George pulls Lennie's ear and sternly tells him to keep away from her. Even simple-minded Lennie has a premonition of danger and "Cried out suddenly, 'I don' like this place, George. This ain't no good place. I wanna get outa here.'" George says they must stay until they get a stake, even though he doesn't like it any better than Lennie. George says, "We can't help it, Lennie." The two men are trapped by their lack of money.

Steinbeck has painted the men and the woman in this novel in their barest, most elemental terms. Lennie, in particular, is described as walking like a bear in the first chapter and drinking like a dog from the pool of water. He has simple, animal instincts and responses: he likes to pet soft things, he admires the beauty of Curley's wife, and he wants to get away from the bad place of the ranch. George admits they are trapped by society. They had to run from the last job because of Lennie's behavior, and now they must stay in this dangerous place because there is nowhere else to go.

This naturalistic portrayal of life—man victimized by his instincts, by society, by the forces of nature, by chance—is balanced primarily by the portraits of Slim and George. Slim recognizes the beauty of Curley's wife without becoming entrapped by it, and he is a recognized authority on everything. He acknowledges the bad with the good and is an example of man at his best. When his bitch has nine pups, he drowns four because she cannot feed all of them. There is no anger or judgment in Slim's decisions, only recognition of necessity. George, through his care of Lennie, is also lifted up out of the bestial. George protects and defends Lennie, even to the point of sacrificing his comfort and well-being. Even though it is unlikely George could ever achieve his dream, he could certainly live more comfortably without Lennie, but he knows Lennie could not survive without someone to take care of him. This caring for the helpless is paralleled by Candy and his old dog. The ancient dog walks lamely, is half blind, and smells. Candy feeds the dog milk because it has no teeth and can't chew. Carlson hates the old dog and can't understand why Candy still keeps it alive. Carlson suggests to Slim that he get Candy to shoot the old dog and give him a pup to raise. Carlson's insensitivity goes to the core of this issue. George and Slim understand that life is measured by more than bare necessity and self-interest; Carlson does not.

Light and dark become symbols for the Manichean cosmos of the ranch. At the beginning of the chapter, the sun "threw a bright dust-laden bar through one of the side windows", and when Curley's wife appears, "the rectangle of sunshine in the doorway was cut off." The forces of good and the forces of evil come into conflict in this novel: there is no light not subdued or cut into bars. Even in Chapter 1, the time of day is evening. This play of light and shadow continues throughout the story.

Chapter 2 continues the theme of loneliness. The boss regards George with suspicion for his connection with Lennie. "Well, I ain't seen one guy take so much trouble for another guy. I just like to know what your interest is." Slim, a loner himself, regards George and Lennie's relationship as unusual among migrant ranch workers. Curley's wife is looking for something, for her husband, or any other man, just as Curley spends much of his time looking for her.

Study Questions

1. Where do the ranch hands keep their personal belongings such as soap, razors and magazines?

2. Candy, the old swamper who shows George and Lennie to their bunks, is missing what limb?

3. What evidence does the old swamper give that the ranch boss is a "pretty nice fella"?

4. What evidence is there that the boss is not a working man?

5. According to the old swamper, what is Curley good at?

6. According to the old swamper, why does Curley wear a work glove on his left hand?

7. What is the general attitude toward Curley's wife?

8. Describe Slim, the jerkline skinner.

9. Why does Carlson suggest shooting Candy's dog?

10. What is the understood question that Lennie wants George to ask Slim?

Answers

1. Each ranch hand keeps his personal items in the apple box nailed over his bunk for that purpose.

2. Candy, the old swamper, is missing a hand.

3. Candy says that the boss brought a whole gallon of whiskey to the men in the bunkhouse for Christmas.

4. The boss wears high-heeled boots and spurs.

5. Candy says Curley is good at boxing.

6. Candy says Curley wears the work glove full of Vaseline to keep his hand soft for his new wife.

7. The men think she is flirting with them. Candy calls her a tart; George calls her a tramp. Lennie thinks she is pretty.

8. Slim is a master craftsman. He is an expert with the mules and his authority is respected more than anyone else's on the ranch.

9. Carlson suggests shooting Candy's dog because it is so old and it stinks.

10. Lennie wants George to ask Slim if Lennie can have one of the puppies Slim's dog has just delivered.

Suggested Essay Topics

1. It seems very unusual for two people in this work, which presents the reader a real slice of life, to have established companions. Consider the pairs presented in this chapter: George and Lennie, Curley and his wife, Candy and his dog. Discuss the relationships involved in the various pairings. What is the basis for each relationship? What are the positive and negative aspects of each?

2. Steinbeck paints a picture of life on the ranch through his characterization, giving the reader important information about them. Compile a list of characters presented by Steinbeck in this chapter and describe the qualities of each. What do the details tell you about each of them? What, in your opinion, does each character represent and why?

SECTION FOUR

Chapter 3

New Characters:

Whit: *one of the common farm hands who also lives in the bunkhouse*

Crooks: *a stable hand*

Summary

Later that same Friday, Slim and George return to the bunkhouse. Outside the other men play horseshoes, while inside Slim and George discuss Lennie. According to George, he and Lennie were born in the same town. George knew Lennie's Aunt Clara who had raised Lennie from infancy. When she died, George became his caregiver. George denies that Lennie is dumb, saying instead that he is simple. He confesses that he played tricks on Lennie in the past but stopped when he realized Lennie's loyalty was so strong that he would do anything George required.

George also tells Slim why he and Lennie left their last job in Weed. Lennie had seen a girl's dress that he thought was pretty, so he reached out to touch it. When he did, the girl began to scream. Lennie panicked, gripped the dress, and wouldn't let go until George hit him in the head with a fence picket. When the girl reported that she had been raped, Lennie was in danger of being lynched, so the two men fled.

When Lennie comes in, hiding a newborn pup that Slim
has given him, George demands that he give it back to its
mother. He explains that Lennie will kill the pup if it isn't
returned to its mother. Slim commends George for his efforts and agrees that Lennie is a "nice fella," a good-hearted
person who "ain't mean," a childlike man.

Candy and his lame dog come in, followed by Carlson, a
ranch hand. After complaining about the smell of the old
dog, Carlson suggests shooting it to put it out of its misery.
Candy refuses, saying that the dog has been his companion
for many years. Carlson presses the issue and will not be put
off by Candy's remonstrances. They are interrupted by Whit,
another ranch hand, who shows them a western magazine
and a letter to the editor written by a man who had worked
on the ranch three months before.

When conversation turns back to Candy's dog, and Slim
agrees with Carlson that the dog is no good to anyone, Candy
yields to the pressure. Carlson, his gun in his pocket, leads
the dog out of the bunk while Candy lies staring at the ceil-
ing. The silence that follows is uncomfortable for all.

After the shot has sounded, Crooks, the stable buck,
comes to the bunkhouse for Slim. The two of them leave to
go to the barn to mend a mule's foot with hot tar.

During a card game with Whit, George is invited to go to
Susie's place, one of the local whorehouses. When Curley
comes looking for his wife, he hints that he is going to confront Slim about her whereabouts. The men in the bunkhouse follow him to the barn to watch the match. George
and Lennie are left in the room. Candy, forgotten, remains
on his bunk facing the wall.

In this private moment, Lennie again prods George to
tell him again of their dream home. Lennie becomes fixated
on tending the rabbits. As George describes the ten-acre
farm, Candy is drawn into their dream. To become a partner

in their dream, he offers to give George $350 of the $600 George says he would need to buy the farm. George agrees. All three are excited at the now realistic prospect of getting the farm.

Obviously irritated, Slim returns to the bunkhouse followed closely by an apologetic Curley. Carlson verbally attacks Curley, calling him "yella as a frog belly." Even Candy adds an insult, mentioning Curley's gloved hand, "Glove fulla vaseline." When Curley turns his glare to Lennie, Lennie is still smiling at the idea of the farm and the rabbits. Curley, however, thinks Lennie is laughing at the insults directed at him.

Curley attacks Lennie, bringing blood from his nose. Then Curley attacks his stomach and cuts off his wind. Lennie cries out and tries to escape. It is only when George has directed him to fight back that Lennie makes a move at Curley. As Curley swings to hit Lennie again, Lennie catches Curley's fist in his own big hand and crushes it. He brings Curley to the floor "flopping like a fish on a line, and his closed fist was lost in Lennie's big hand."

When George finally gets Lennie to release Curley, his hand is mutilated. Lennie is miserable, insisting that he didn't want to hurt anybody, and George is afraid that the boss will fire him and Lennie. Slim convinces Curley not to rat on Lennie, telling him to say he got his hand stuck in a machine. If not, he and the men will tell what really happened and everyone will laugh at Curley.

Lennie's only concern is that George won't let him tend the rabbits on their dream ranch because of what he did to Curley. George reassures him that he didn't do anything wrong.

Analysis

Chapter 3 focuses on relationships, the code of conduct observed by the migrant ranch workers and their values.

Their heroes come from the Western magazines that they read and accumulate. These heroes, unlike themselves, are always champions, triumphing over every situation. Though the tales in the magazines are unreal, and something the ranch men publicly scoff at, they offer heroes in whom the men secretly believe. Whit introduces the Western magazines to the story, and it is Slim who most symbolizes the heroes they portray.

When George and Slim discuss Lennie, George speaks of him "proudly," as if he were George's child. Then, with Slim's "Godlike eyes fastened on him," George makes his "confession" of the cruel jokes he has played on Lennie in the past. Even when he beat him, Lennie never got mad or lifted his hand against George. He describes one incident to demonstrate Lennie's devotion to him.

> "One day a bunch of guys was standin' around up on the Sacramento River. I was feelin' pretty smart. I turns to Lennie and says, 'Jump in.' An' he jumps. Couldn't swim a stroke. He damn near drowned before we could get him. An' he was so damn nice to me for pullin' him out. Clean forgot I told him to jump in. Well, I ain't done nothing like that no more."

The loneliness of a migrant worker's life is echoed in George's words:

> "I ain't got no people.... I seen the guys that go around on the ranches alone. That ain't no good. They don't have no fun. After a long time they get mean. They get wantin' to fight all the time."

But his special relationship with Lennie has a price. According to George, Lennie's "a God damn nuisance most of the time...because he's so dumb."

His growing confidence in Slim enables George to confess to him what had happened in Weed that forced them to move on. Slim makes no judgments. With his eyes level and unwinking, he again absolves Lennie of any wrongdoing, saying, "He ain't mean....I can tell a mean guy a mile off." As if to reinforce this simplicity and innocence, Lennie enters the bunkhouse beaming with delight, holding the brown and white pup Slim has given him.

Lennie tries to conceal the pup against his stomach, but George grabs Lennie and removes the tiny newborn pup. George explains to Lennie that the pup must sleep with its mother or it will die. When Lennie leaves for the barn, Slim comments, "He's jes' like a kid." George bets that Lennie will sleep out in the barn by the dogs.

Lennie's childlike, inherently good nature, and George's power over him are displayed when Curley attacks him later that Friday night. Though Curley has pounded Lennie's face, Lennie still stands with his hands at his side calling to George for help. Only when George has given Lennie the command does the hulking man make any sort of move at Curley. Lennie, even then, does not unleash a ferocious anger; he simply stops Curley's fist and holds it. He does not mean for Curley's fist to be crushed; he simply does not know his own strength. Even when the fight has ended, Lennie is crying to George that he "didn't wanta hurt him." Lennie hasn't been angry, only scared.

Steinbeck draws a parallel between George and Lennie and the crippled Candy and his old dog. Like George, who watches over Lennie, Candy is the custodian of a sick and lame dog that has outlived its usefulness. But his dog is the one thing the lonely stable swamper has that passes for a

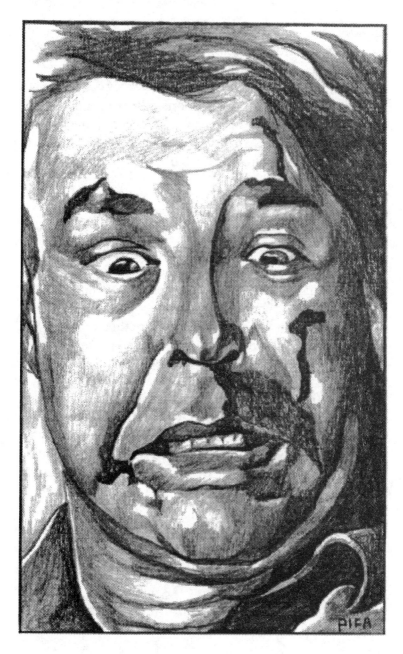

friend. Carlson's shooting of the dog with his Luger foreshadows the scene between George and Lennie in the final chapter. "I ought to of shot that dog myself," he tells George. "I
shouldn't ought to of let no stranger shoot my dog." Candy's
regret is that he shirked his responsibility to his old friend
and violated the code of conduct. Now completely alone,
Candy is drawn into George and Lennie's dream. Desperately
he offers them his hard-earned bankroll of $350.

> "Maybe if I give you guys my money, you'll
> let me hoe in the garden even after I ain't no
> good at it. An' I'll wash dishes an' little
> chicken stuff like that. But I'll be on our own
> place…. You seen what they done to my dog
> tonight? They says he wasn't no good to him-
> self nor nobody else. When they can me here
> I wisht somebody'd shoot me. But they won't
> do nothing like that. I won't have no place to
> go, an' I can't get no more jobs."

Another example of the code that governs the lives of
these men can be seen in Curley's response to having his
hand crushed by Lennie. Rather than admit he was bested
by another man, he chooses to lie and say that it was caught
in a machine. Slim, the quiet Western hero, comes to the
rescue of George and Lennie.

> "I think you got your han' caught in a ma-
> chine. If you don't tell nobody what hap-
> pened, we ain't going to. But you jus tell an'
> try to get this guy canned and we'll tell
> ever'body, an' then will you get the laugh."

Crushing Curley's hand creates problems for the future. Now Curley hates Lennie and would enjoy seeing him destroyed. It is just a matter of time.

There is sufficient symbolism in this chapter to foreshadow Lennie's and George's fate. The chapter opens with evening brightness outside the bunkhouse but darkness inside. Even turning on the tin-shaded electric light above the card table merely creates an oasis of light, leaving the bunk house "still in the dark." George plays solitaire with a deliberate slowness after Carlton shoots Candy's old dog. The game symbolizes his ultimate state of solitude, as well as the naturalistic forces of chance and fate. Lennie reaches for a face card and wants to know why "both ends are the same," and George says that's just the way the cards are made. Finally, Lennie is afraid the fight with Curley, even though not his fault, will be grounds for not letting him tend the rabbits.

Throughout the first part of the novel, no one thinks the farm will become a reality, if the farm even exists. But describing the farm is like a mantra. George's voice becomes "warmer" when describing their ten acres: shack, chicken run, orchard, pig pen, smoke house, river with salmon, vegetable garden, and assorted animals, including Lennie's beloved rabbits. However, details add unreality to the dream: catching a hundred salmon, cream so thick it must be cut with a knife, selling a few eggs for whiskey money, and not having to work hard more than six or seven hours a day. When Candy offers to pitch in his money, the men fall silent. "They looked at one another, amazed. This thing they had never really believed in was coming true." During the time of drifting, George and Lennie had comforted themselves with an unrealistic dream. Now, perhaps, with the help of Candy, the three misfits can escape the cruel society in which they live. The hope is short-lived.

Study Questions

1. Why does George say Lennie will want to sleep in the barn that Friday night?

2. According to George, how did he end up traveling with Lennie?

3. What happened that made George stop playing dirty tricks on Lennie?

4. Why did George and Lennie have to flee from Weed?

5. Who makes the final decision on whether or not Candy's old dog should be shot?

6. What is significant about the letter Whit reads from the Western magazine?

7. Why does George agree to let Candy come with them to their dream farm?

8. Why does Curley attack Lennie in the bunk house?

9. Why does Curley agree not to get Lennie fired for crushing his hand?

10. What punishment does Lennie fear he will get for hurting Curley?

Answers

1. George says Lennie will want to sleep with the puppy Slim has said Lennie can have when it is weaned.

2. George says that he and Lennie are both from Auburn and that he knew Lennie's Aunt Clara who raised him. He says that when the aunt died Lennie had just come along with him to work.

3. The last time George played a trick on Lennie, he told Lennie to jump into a river and Lennie did even though he couldn't swim. Before George got him out, he al-

most drowned. Lennie, however, was thankful to George for getting him out instead of angry for telling him to jump in.

4. George says that he and Lennie had to flee from Weed because Lennie was accused of trying to rape a girl there. In fact, he had only been trying to feel the dress she was wearing.

5. Slim is the one who makes the final decision.

6. The letter was written by a former ranch hand they had known.

7. Candy offers to give George $350, his life's savings, if they will let him come along. With his money they should be able to buy the farm at the end of the next month so George agrees to let him in on their dream.

8. Curley attacks Lennie because he thinks Lennie is laughing at him after Carlson has called him "yella as a frog belly." In fact, Lennie is smiling at the idea in his head of their farm.

9. Slim convinces Curley that if he tells, everyone will laugh at him for getting beaten up by a retarded man.

10. George has told Lennie that he will not let Lennie tend the rabbits if he does one more bad thing. Lennie is afraid this will be that bad thing.

Suggested Essay Topics

1. Trace the parallels that are developed between Candy and his dog and George and his companion. Consider the amount of time they have spent together, the way they view the limitations of their companions, the way they defend their companions, and any other points of similarity you see.

2. George and Lennie's plan to buy a ranch in the first chapter is nothing more than an unattainable dream. How does it become a more concrete plan in the second chapter, and what is the role that Candy plays in taking this dream closer to reality?

Chapter 4

Summary

Chapter 4 takes place on the following Saturday night. It is set in the tidy room of Crooks, the Negro stable buck, who tends to the horses and mends the leather items used with the animals. His room, a shed built against the wall of the barn, is decorated in much the same way as the bunkhouse, except he keeps in his room his leather working tools and medicines. His room also contains more personal items, including books. He has a dictionary and a copy of the California civil code. Crooks is himself crooked, bent to the left by a crooked spine. Steinbeck describes him as a "proud, aloof man," who keeps his distance and demands that the others on the ranch keep theirs.

Crooks is sitting on his bed rubbing medicine onto his back when Lennie appears at his doorway, smiling. He explains that he has come into the barn to look at his puppy. He says that the others have gone into town and that he has gotten lonely. Though Crooks is at first reluctant to have one of the white farm hands in his room, he eventually yields.

Crooks decides aloud that Lennie is completely crazy and that Lennie often doesn't understand and can't remember what George talks about. He recognizes, too, the need of one man to have the company of another, even if it is just someone to talk to, who can't understand completely.

Enjoying his intellectual superiority over Lennie, Crooks begins to taunt him, telling him to imagine that George never came back, and asking Lennie what he'd do. Lennie, not understanding, thinks that someone has hurt George and becomes angry. Crooks calms him and explains that he was just trying to make Lennie see how lonely things are for the only black man on the ranch. He cries to Lennie, telling him that books are not enough; reading doesn't take the place of the companionship he is denied simply because of his color.

Lennie remains oblivious to Crooks's point and returns, instead, to the dream of the two men to buy their farm. Crooks is scornful, saying that he's seen hundreds of men come along with the same dream.

When Candy enters the barn looking for Lennie, Crooks calls him into his room. Candy, a little embarrassed, enters and comments that this is the first time he's ever been in Crooks's room even though they have both been there for a long time.

Sufficiently recovered, and prompted by Lennie, Candy returns to his original topic, the rabbits they will have on their farm. Crooks interrupts to add that their dream is an impossible one that he has seen shattered every time.

Candy defends their dream, telling Crooks that they already have the needed money in the bank. Crooks becomes drawn into the potential of this dream-about-to-become-a-reality, and he offers to work for free if they will just let him in on it.

At this moment, Curley's wife enters. Lennie stares at her, fascinated by her beauty. Curley and Crooks scowl at her, and then each, in turn, encourages her to leave. She resists, arguing that she too should have someone she can talk to. Candy flares and stands up, insisting that she leave. He declares he is not afraid of her trying to get them fired, because they have a farm of their own to go to. She laughs, saying

that she's seen lots of men with that dream. Candy returns her derisive laugh and declares that the men will not talk to her.

Curley's wife then turns her attention to Lennie, asking him where the bruises on his face came from. Candy becomes angry and threatens to tell George on her.

Crooks stands up with Candy and tells Curley's wife that she has no business there and he insists that she leave his room. Curley's wife turns on him, scornful, and reminds him that she can easily have him hanged. It is enough to crush Crooks and he submits completely. Candy returns the threat, saying that they would reveal that she had set him up. She retaliates, saying that nobody would believe them. Candy concedes that she is right.

Candy is finally successful in getting her to leave by telling her that he hears the men returning from town.

When she slips out, Crooks asks the others to go. Candy speaks up, saying that Curley's wife has no business speaking to him that way. Crooks, though, remains in his completely submissive state.

George, coming into the barn looking for Lennie, is hailed into Crooks's room. He openly objects to Lennie being in Crooks's room. When Candy begins to tell George about the figuring he's been doing about their farm, George stops him, reminding him that he was to tell no one.

George orders the two men out of Crooks's room. As the three men are leaving, Crooks, having been reminded of his place as a black man among whites, calls out to Candy and tells him to forget his offer to work for them for free. He says that he had only been joking about wanting to go with them to their farm.

The chapter ends, as it began, with Crooks sitting on his bed rubbing his back with liniment.

Analysis

This chapter focuses on the four lonely misfits: Crooks, Lennie, Candy, and Curley's wife. Crooks is crippled physically, made crooked by his twisted spine. He is socially alienated by his color and emotionally detached by his isolation. He lives alone, with a manure pile under his window and no one to talk to. He can't even play cards with the others in the bunkhouse because he is black and the men say he stinks. When Lennie comes to his door looking for companionship, Crooks first tries to send him away, but Lennie is not easily dismissed. With George gone to the whorehouse Lennie is lonely, just as Crooks is secretly lonely, although the hurt Crooks feels prevents him from admitting his loneliness.

After a while Crooks decides that it is safe to talk to Lennie, since Lennie is obviously "crazy as a wedge." He tells Lennie about his childhood, revealing his days as a boy on a chicken ranch, playing with the white kids. He gets excited about the idea of having someone to listen to him. But Lennie doesn't understand him, and he isn't even listening. He is more concerned about the puppies in the barn and the rabbits they're going to get. Envious of Lennie's relationship with George, Crooks teases and torments him. He asks Lennie to imagine that George has left him for good, that he got hurt, and that Lennie will never see his friend George again. Crooks takes pleasure in his torture of the frightened Lennie. "Want me ta tell ya what'll happen?" he asks Lennie. "They'll take ya to the booby hatch. They'll tie ya up with a collar, like a dog." But when he sees the danger of upsetting Lennie, he reassures him that George will return.

Lennie does not readily understand, so the lonely Crooks explains that just playing horseshoes in the evening and then coming in to nothing but books isn't enough.

"You got George. You know he's goin' to come
back. S'pose you didn't have nobody. Sure
you could play horseshoes till it got dark, but
then you got to read books. Books ain't no
good. A guy needs somebody - to be near
him." He whined, "A guy goes nuts if he ain't
got nobody....a guy gets too lonely an' he gets
sick."

When the misfit Candy enters Crooks's room, Crooks
finds it "difficult...to conceal his pleasure with anger." As if
to emphasize Crooks's isolation, Candy comments that although both he and Crooks have been on the ranch a long
time, he has never been in Crooks's room.

With his dog gone, we see that Lennie and George have
become Candy's "somebody." Candy knows that Lennie will
not understand the figuring he has done about making a
profit from the rabbits, but it doesn't matter. Candy needs
their dream of getting a ranch, and he needs Lennie as an
audience.

The crippled Crooks is temporarily strengthened when
he is taken into the confidences of these two white ranch
hands. He talks to them simply as other men, worthy of their
confidences regarding the dream farm. He goes so far as
admitting that he wants a part of their dream. They even
consider letting him join them there.

Their plans are interrupted when Curley's wife, the big-
gest misfit of them all, comes into the barn. Her face is
heavily made up and her lips slightly parted. She is breath-
ing hard as though she has been running. Deprived of her
husband, who has gone with the others to the whorehouse,
she, too, is looking for one thing: companionship. But Crooks
and Candy make her unwelcome and she confronts them.
For all of her inexperience and lack of education, she is perceptive and she shows a deep insight into things.

> "Funny thing... If I catch any one man, and
> he's alone, I get along fine with him. But just
> let two of the guys get together an you won't
> talk. Jus' nothing but mad.... You're all scared
> of each other, that's what."

The men do not sympathize with Curley's wife. They do not take her into their circle, but insist repeatedly that she leave.

> "I ain't giving you no trouble. Think I don't
> like to talk to somebody ever' once in a while?
> Think I like to stick in that house alla time?"

She is disenchanted with her husband, who "Spends all his time sayin' what he's gonna do to guys he don't like, and he don't like nobody." She is so desperate for company that she has to come out to the barn to talk to the weak ones that the others left behind, "a bunch of bindle stiffs — a nigger an' a dum-dum and a lousy ol' sheep—an likin' it because they ain't nobody else."

She presses Lennie for an explanation of the bruises on his face and correctly guesses that he was the cause of Curley's broken hand. "I'm glad you bust up Curley a little bit. He got it comin' to him. Sometimes I'd like to bust him myself."

Imbued with a newfound strength, Crooks stands up to Curley's wife, as Candy does. Crooks, though, is immediately whipped back down. She brandishes in his face her power to take his life. She reminds him, "Nigger, I could have you strung up on a tree so easy it ain't even funny." Not even Candy can deny that she could have Crooks lynched on a whim.

Thoroughly beaten back into his socially crippled stage, Crooks tells the men to leave his room with the manure pile outside. He may not enjoy his rights—rights to isolation—but they are at least his. When George returns to find Lennie, Crooks even retracts his request to join the men on their dream farm. He instead finds comfort in the routine of his old life, a life of pain and liniment.

Evidence of man's essential cruelty appears in this chapter. Crooks baits Lennie with the idea that George might never come back; only when Lennie becomes threatening does Crooks back off and placate the frightened Lennie. Curley's wife admits feelings of hostility toward her husband and laughs at the idea of the farm. "I seen too many of you guys. If you had two bits in the worl', why you'd be in gettin' two shots of corn with it and suckin' the bottom of the glass." When Curley's wife says she might get some rabbits of her own, Crooks knows that she has no "rights messing around here at all." In trying to protect Lennie, Crooks opens himself to attack. Curley's wife viciously turns on Crooks and threatens him because he is a "Nigger" who cannot afford to open his "trap." When Candy says he will tell if she tries to frame Crooks, she replies, "Nobody'd listen to you."

Study Questions

1. Why has Crooks been able to accumulate more personal items than the other ranch hands?

2. What reason does Crooks first give for Lennie not being welcome in his room?

3. According to Crooks, why does a person need a companion?

4. What is Crooks's initial response to Candy's account of the dream farm and what evidence is there that his attitude changes?

5. According to Curley's wife, why are the men afraid to talk to her when there is more than one present?

6. Why doesn't Curley's wife like talking to her husband?

7. What reason does Candy give when he says that they are no longer afraid that Curley's wife will get them fired?

8. What makes Crooks so bold as to confront Curley's wife and tell her to leave his room?

9. How does Candy finally make Curley's wife leave the barn?

10. What does George say about Candy and Lennie visiting with Crooks?

Answers

1. Because of the type of job he has and because Crooks is crippled, he is more permanent than the other men, so he can accumulate personal items without having to worry about how he will carry them with him to the next job.

2. Crooks says at first that Lennie is not welcome in his room because Crooks is not welcome in the bunkhouse.

3. Crooks says that a person who stays alone too long goes "nuts."

4. Crooks says that the dream will never materialize. He says he has seen hundreds of men chasing the same dream and never catching it. But when he hears that they have the money for the farm in the bank, he becomes more convinced and even offers to work for free if they will let him come with them.

5. Curley's wife says that the men are "scared of each other... scared the rest is goin' to get something on you."

6. Curley's wife doesn't like talking to her husband because all he ever wants to talk about is beating up people.

7. Candy explains that they are no longer afraid because they now have somewhere else to go—their own farm.

8. He forgets his own limitations as a black man of the 1930s because Lennie and Candy have come in and treated him as an equal. For a moment, he later explains, he forgot how powerless he really is there.

9. Candy gets Curley's wife to leave the barn by telling her that he has heard the other men returning from town.

10. George tells them that they should not be in Crooks's room and that they should not have told him about the farm.

Suggested Essay Topics

1. Several characters have suggested a need to have a companion or just a person who will listen. What evidence is given here that this is a strong desire of many of the characters? Consider, too, the effect that having a companion gives to Candy and Crooks as they confront Curley's wife.

2. Crooks, Lennie, Candy, and Curley's wife are lonely people with specific needs. Compare the four characters and discuss what they need and want to end their respective feelings of loneliness.

Chapter 5

Summary

Chapter 5 takes place in the barn on the following Sunday afternoon. As the men are playing horseshoes outside, Lennie sits alone in the barn. He is thinking and worrying about his dead puppy, upset that he accidentally killed it even though he didn't bounce it very hard. He debates with himself over whether this is a bad thing. It is not bad enough to mean he must go and hide at the clearing, but it may be bad enough to make George so mad he won't let Lennie tend the rabbits when they buy their ranch. Deciding that George will be angry, he throws the puppy across the barn. Shortly thereafter he retrieves the puppy and buries it in the hay.

When Curley's wife comes into the barn, Lennie declares that he will not talk to her because George has told him not to. If he does, Lennie will not be allowed to take care of the rabbits. Curley's wife stays, saying that she just wants someone to talk to, and she insists that the others won't be mad because they will not know.

With Lennie listening, she tells him in detail how she could have been an actress in the movies. She even confesses, as she hasn't before, that she doesn't like her husband.

Lennie, stroking his puppy throughout her discourse, shows no signs of listening to her. When she finishes talking, he begins speaking on the subject which has occupied

his mind, escaping punishment for killing the puppy and being allowed to tend the rabbits.

Curley's wife asks him why he likes rabbits so much. He tells her that he likes to pet them because they are so soft. She says that she feels the same way about silk and velvet. Deciding aloud that he is "nuts" but "like a big baby," she takes Lennie's hand and lets him stroke her soft hair.

When he strokes harder, she angrily tells him not to mess it up. As she tries to jerk her head away, he closes his fingers and hangs on to her hair. In a panic to silence her scream, he closes his hand over her mouth, asking her to please be quiet, so George won't be mad and forbid him to tend the rabbits. With one hand over her face and the other at the back of her head, he shakes her. When he lays her on the ground, she is still and quiet. He has broken her neck. He realizes that she is dead and that he has done another bad thing. He covers her partly with hay. Listening to the men at horseshoes, he remembers that George has told him to go back to the river and wait in the bushes if something like this happens. Taking the puppy with him, he sneaks out of the barn.

After Lennie has left, Candy comes into the barn looking for him. Instead he finds Curley's wife. He runs out again and comes back with George. George realizes what has happened and says that they will have to tell the others and have Lennie locked up since he'd starve out on his own. Candy suggests letting Lennie escape since Curley will want him lynched. George agrees that the others will want Lennie lynched. Both men recognize that their dream of the ranch is dead along with Curley's wife.

Declaring that he will not let the men hurt Lennie, George tells Candy that he is going back to the bunkhouse. Candy is to give George some time to return to the bunkhouse and then go tell the others about Curley's wife. George

is going to act as if he didn't already know. When George is gone, Candy curses Curley's dead wife for messing up everything.

Following their plan, Candy calls the men into the barn. Curley at once decides that Lennie is responsible. Showing more concern for getting Lennie than for his dead wife, Curley and Carlson go for their guns. Slim, left alone with George in the barn, convinces George that locking Lennie up would be no better an alternative than what Curley and Carlson have planned.

When Carlson returns, he announces that his pistol is gone and proclaims that Lennie has taken it. Arranging quickly for another gun, and for someone to get the deputy sheriff, Curley asks George whether he plans to join in the chase. George agrees to come, but he asks if they can just try to catch Lennie without killing him. Curley refuses emphatically.

The chapter closes, as it opened, in the still barn.

Analysis

Foreshadowing plays an important part in the story. From the dead mouse in Chapter 1, Steinbeck prepares the reader for death. He uses foreshadowing again as Chapter 5 unfolds. Once again Lennie has unintentionally killed something he wants desperately to keep alive—the brown and white puppy. He is terribly sorry, not because he really understands that his actions have caused another death, but because he fears that the worst possible thing will happen: George will be mad and will follow through on his promise not to let Lennie tend the rabbits.

Lennie is still absorbed in these thoughts while Curley's wife is confiding in him. He has no interest in the woman and views her only as a threat to his dream of tending the rabbits. Just as Crooks had said to Lennie, she expresses the strong need to have an audience, a companion who will listen. When she finally gets Lennie still, "her words tumbled out in a passion of communication, as though she hurried before her listener could be taken away."

Like the others on the ranch she has her own dream which she tries to share, her lost dream of being an actress. "I coulda made somethin' of myself," she tells him. "Maybe I will yet." She describes her chance at age 15 to leave town with a traveling show: "If I went, I wouldn't be livin' like this, you bet."

But Lennie is not attentive to her desperation. She even has to ask him if he's listening. Still, she goes on to confide in him something she "ain't told...to nobody before," —that she doesn't like her husband. She hurriedly married him only after she didn't get a letter from Hollywood. Her observation is that Curley "ain't a nice fella." Just as Crooks, she feels most comfortable with Lennie, after she decides that he is too crazy to remember all that she says so that it couldn't possibly be used against her. But Lennie's only concern is the dead puppy.

"Maybe," he says to her, "if I took this pup out and throwed him away George wouldn't never know. An' then I could tend the rabbits without no trouble."

As something of a reward for his willingness to listen, she lets him stroke her hair. Ironically, Lennie doesn't reach for her hair. Instead it is Curley's wife who puts his hand on her head.

> He moved his hand a little and her hoarse cry came out. Then Lennie grew angry. "Now don't," he said. "I don't want you to yell. You gonna get me in trouble jus' like George says you will.... Don't you go yellin'," he said, and he shook her; and her body flopped like a fish. And then she was still, for Lennie had broken her neck.

As with the puppy and the many mice before, Lennie unintentionally kills the pretty, soft thing he wanted to pet. With this one act, the death of Curley's wife, comes the climax of the story, and it brings with it the death of all their dreams.

Candy's concern, when he brings George to see Curley's wife's body, is in part about Lennie. But his "greatest fear" is that their dream will die. He asks George if they can still pursue the dream, but for George the dream is already dead. As Candy watches George go, his sorrow and his anger grow into words.

> "You God damn tramp," he said viciously.
> "You done it, di'n't you? I s'pose you're glad.
> Ever'body knowed you'd mess things up. You
> wasn't no good. You ain't no good now, you
> lousy tart…. I could of hoed in the garden and
> washed dishes for them guys."

When Candy is "blinded with tears," they are tears for the death of the dream, not for the death of Curley's wife or for the approaching death of Lennie.

To George the dream only existed as part of his relationship with Lennie. With Lennie's imminent end, his and George's dream farm is tossed on to the refuse heap with all of the other hundreds of similar ranch hands' dreams. As Crooks and Curley's wife had predicted, this dream, like the others, will not come true.

When the others come in, George tries to find a way to keep Lennie alive. Just as Candy had argued to keep his old, crippled dog alive, George searches for a way to keep his friend alive. He asks Slim if they couldn't just lock him away, instead of killing him. Slim tells George what he already knows, that locking Lennie away will be even worse. Death at the hands of Curley will be equally bad, for Curley, intent

on revenge, more for his shattered hand than for his dead wife, wants Lennie to suffer. "I'm gonna shoot the guts outa that big bastard myself, even if I only got one hand. I'm gonna get 'im." George's only real choice is to handle Lennie's death himself.

The sympathy Candy expresses as George and the other men begin their pursuit of Lennie could be for either of his friends. When he says softly "Poor bastard," he may be referring to Lennie. He has said Lennie is "such a nice fella," and he knows that Lennie will now be hunted down and shot for an act he did not intend to commit. But Candy may also be referring to George, whom he knows will lose a faithful companion, just as Candy himself had done just two days before. As he did when his own pet was about to be shot, Candy lies down, now in the barn, awaiting the sound of the gun. He understands how George feels about the approaching death of Lennie.

Steinbeck uses the interplay of light and dark as well as movement inside the barn to symbolize the tragedy as it happens. When the chapter opens, the afternoon sun "sliced" through cracks in the barn wall and "lay in bright lines on the hay." When Curley's wife enters and speaks to Lennie, the sun is going down and the sun streaks are over the heads of the horses. After Lennie breaks her neck, Curley's wife lies half-covered with hay in light that "was growing soft." She appears very pretty and simple. Steinbeck writes that a moment settles and appears to hold still, then sluggishly moves on. Candy discovers the body and runs out to get George, but the barn is "alive now" with the disturbed movement of the horses. As the men all leave to find Lennie, Candy is left in the barn that is "darkening gradually" with the horses shifting in their stalls. Candy covers his eyes with his arm.

Study Questions

1. What has happened to Lennie's puppy and why?

2. What two pieces of information does Curley's wife share with Lennie?

3. Why does Curley's wife offer to let Lennie caress her hair?

4. How and why does Lennie kill Curley's wife?

5. Why does George say that they can't let Lennie escape to live on his own?

6. What is Candy's greatest fear?

7. When George asks Slim about just trying to catch Lennie instead of killing him, what advice does Slim give George?

8. What makes the men think that Lennie is armed?

9. Where does Curley plan to aim if he shoots Lennie?

10. Who stays with Curley's wife as the others go off in pursuit of Lennie?

Answers

1. Lennie has killed his puppy by bouncing it too hard.

2. Curley's wife tells him about her dream to be an ac-tress, and she tells him her secret that she does not like Curley.

3. Curley's wife says that she shares Lennie's fondness of soft things and since she regards him as "a big baby," she sees no harm in letting him feel the softness of her hair.

4. Lennie kills Curley's wife by breaking her neck because he is shaking her, trying to make her be quiet so he won't get into trouble.

5. George says that Lennie will starve out on his own.

6. Candy's greatest fear is that they will not get the farm.

7. Slim tells George that if they just catch Lennie, he would be strapped down and caged, which would be worse than death.

8. The men think that Lennie is armed because Carlson comes into the barn and announces that his gun is missing.

9. Curley is planning to shoot Lennie in the stomach.

10. Candy stays with Curley's wife.

Suggested Essay Topics

1. After Candy has brought George to the barn to show him Curley's wife, George leaves and Candy cries. What is the true source of Candy's sadness and why? Compare the killing of Curley's wife to the night Candy's old dog was shot and killed by Carlson.

2. Death is the beginning and the culminating event in the chapter, but the killing of Curley's wife is regarded with a lack of emotion by the characters, even less than the killing of the puppy or the shooting of Candy's dog earlier in the book. Why do you think this is so? Why is the moral issue of her murder, the question of right and wrong, never really an issue when Curley's wife's body is discovered by the men?

SECTION SEVEN

Chapter 6

Summary

This final chapter takes place where the first chapter began, at the green pool of the Salinas River in the late afternoon. As before, Lennie comes to the sandy clearing and goes to the pool to drink.

Sitting on the bank Lennie begins to hallucinate and he talks to his dead Aunt Clara who had raised him. She scolds him, saying the same things George has always said to him at such times. When she disappears, a gigantic rabbit takes her place. It tells Lennie that he isn't worthy of tending rabbits. It tells him that George is going to beat him and leave him. When George comes out of the brush, the rabbit too disappears.

Lennie, at once, confesses that he has done a bad thing and invites George to scold him. George tries, but only with Lennie's prompting finishes, going through their usual routine.

When George hears the men closing in on them, he tells Lennie to look across the river. As he describes for the last time the farm that he and Lennie have so long dreamed of, he lifts Carlson's gun from his side pocket. With great difficulty he points it at the back of Lennie's head, and as his hand shakes violently, George pulls the trigger.

The men then quickly come out of the brush to join him in the clearing. Slim comes over to where George is sitting and sits beside him, consoling him.

Carlson asks how it happened. George lies and says that he took the gun from Lennie and shot him with it.

Slim, still at George's side, says again that George only did what he had to do. The two of them depart up the same trail that had first brought George and Lennie into this clearing. Curley and Carlson are left standing in the clearing watching them go.

Analysis

Completing their cycle, George and Lennie end this journey where they started it, back at the pond. As it was in the beginning when they arrived, it is the end of day, late afternoon in a "pleasant shade" by the "deep green" pool of the Salinas River. Symbolically, Steinbeck describes a water snake being eaten by a heron. As the "tail waved frantically" down the heron's beak, a strong gust of wind makes waves in the surface of the water and drives through the tops of the trees. When the wind dies down, the heron is awaiting the arrival of another snake swimming in the water, but the bird flies off because Lennie arrives.

Steinbeck parallels the action of the beginning, but there are contrasts. In the opening chapter Lennie walks heavily, dragging his feet the way a bear drags his paws. He drops his blankets and flings himself down to drink with long gulps, "snorting into the water like a horse." After he drinks, he dabbles his fingers in the water and splashes it. Then, he imitates George by sitting with his knees drawn up and embraced by his arms. In the opening, Lennie can be noisy, thoughtless, and heedless, secure in the knowledge that George is there to take care of him. It is a sharp contrast to the ending of the novel in which Lennie's actions are quieter and betray his fear of being caught.

In this scene at the end, Lennie comes quietly to the pool's edge and barely touches his lips to the water. When a bird skitters over the dry leaves, Lennie's head jerks up, and he does not finish drinking until he spots the bird. Then, he sits on the bank so he can watch the trail's entrance. He sits embracing his knees with his arms, waiting for George to come, but this time George cannot rescue him.

When Lennie is visited by the hallucinations of his dead Aunt Clara and the gigantic rabbit, they speak to him in his voice. With these characters he chastises himself, saying the things that George would normally say. Though the comments are negative and harsh, they are still comforting. Lennie knows that when George says those things he doesn't really mean them. In fact, George has said them so often to Lennie that they have become part of a routine response, and the routine itself has become a comfort.

George has deliberately misdirected the others in pursuit of Lennie so that he could come back to this predetermined meeting place. He has brought Carlson's gun because he knows there is no escape for Lennie. Even if he could take Lennie and run, he knows they will be pursued until they are caught. Although they were not followed after the incident at Weed because it had not been as severe, the murder of Curley's wife is inescapable for them.

In this situation, George has only two choices. Either he can let Curley and Carlson shoot Lennie, or he can do it himself. George is now in the same position Candy had been in with the old dog that he had loved so much. But Candy had let someone else, a stranger, end his companion's life and he regretted it, and George is determined not to make that same mistake. If it has to be done, George will do it himself. Lennie means that much to him.

With great difficulty George fires the gun at the place where Carlson had told Candy to shoot the dog, the spot at

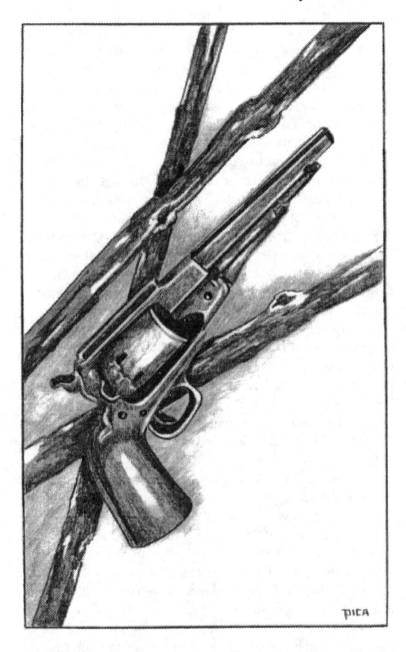

which the creature would die feeling no pain. George pulls the trigger only after taking Lennie to their dream farm one last time.

With Lennie dead, George sits on the river bank. There is no question of morality as Slim, the God-like, respected ranch hand, comes directly to George's side and sits down. He tells George that he did what was right, what had to be done. Slim understands completely and he consoles George. "Slim twitched George's elbow. 'Come on, George. Me an' you'll go an' get a drink.'"

The others do not understand the drama that has occurred, and even if they knew the truth, they could never understand why George had to do it. "Now what the hell ya suppose is eatin' them two guys?" Carlson asks. Just like the typical "bindle stiff" will never share the devotion of another, Curley and Carlson cannot understand the loss George grieves.

Study Questions

1. What scenes of death does Steinbeck describe in the beginning of Chapter 6 that parallel the events of the previous chapter and foreshadow the event to come?

2. How does the chapter bring the book full circle?

3. What two imaginary visitors does Lennie have while sitting on the river bank?

4. What is the subject of the conversation Lennie has with his first visitor?

5. What does his second visitor tell Lennie that recalls an earlier conversation he had with Crooks?

6. How is George and Lennie's conversation similar to the one that they had by the pool in Chapter 1?

7. Where has George gotten the gun he takes from his

front pocket while sitting with Lennie on the river bank?

8. What evidence is there that George is having a terribly difficult time bringing himself to shoot Lennie?

9. What lie does George tell about the way Lennie died?

10. What evidence is there that Slim understands what has really happened there on the river bank?

Answers

1. A water snake gliding in the pool is caught by a heron and eaten while its tail waves frantically, and a strong wind blows into the clearing and dies down.

2. The book begins and ends at the pool by the clearing.

3. While sitting by the clearing Lennie is visited by a hallucination of his Aunt Clara and of a gigantic rabbit.

4. Aunt Clara accuses Lennie of doing bad things. She tells him how George is always doing nice things for Lennie and taking care of him.

5. The rabbit tells Lennie that George isn't going to let Lennie tend the rabbits and that he's going to beat him with a stick. Like Crooks, the gigantic rabbit says that George is going to leave Lennie and never come back.

6. As in the first chapter, George tells Lennie how easy his life would be if he was alone. And Lennie tells George that he will run off to the hills and find a cave to live in by himself.

7. George has taken the gun he has from Carlson's bunk.

8. The first time George raises the gun to the back of Lennie's head, he can't pull the trigger and lays the gun down again. The second time, when he does fire the

gun, his hand is shaking violently.

9. George lets the men believe that he took the gun from Lennie and then shot him in the same attitude as they would have.

10. Slim shows that he understands what George has done as he consoles George and tells him that he has only done what he had to do.

Suggested Essay Topics

1. When George shoots Lennie, is this a sign of the strength of his love or the weakness of his love for Lennie? Has he finally followed through on the threat to abandon Lennie? Why does he shoot Lennie in the middle of their imagining the farm one last time?

2. Murder is a crime, in some states punishable by death. By all definitions, George plans and carries out the murder of his best friend. But there seems to be no concern for taking a human life. Why do you think this is so? When, if anytime, do you think it would be justified?

Sample Analytical Paper Topics

The following analytical paper topics are designed to test your understanding of this novel as a whole and to analyze important themes and literary devices. Following each question is a sample outline to help you get started.

Topic #1

Loneliness is a dominant theme in *Of Mice and Men*. Most of the characters are lonely and searching for someone who can serve as a companion or just as an audience. Discuss the examples of character loneliness, the efforts of the characters in search of companionship, and their varying degrees of success.

Outline

I. Thesis statement: *In his novel* Of Mice and Men, *Steinbeck depicts the essential loneliness of California ranch life in the 1930s. He illustrates how people are driven to find companionship.*

II. Absence of character names

   A. The Boss

   B. Curley's wife

III. George and Lennie

    A. Consider each other family

    B. Lennie described as a kind of pet

    C. George's philosophy about workers who travel alone

    D. The Godlike Slim as George's audience

IV. Candy

    A. Candy's attachment to his dog

    B. The death of his dog

    C. His request to join George and Lennie

    D. His need to share his thoughts with Lennie

V. Crooks

    A. Isolated by his skin color

    B. His eagerness for company

    C. His desire to share the dream of the farm

VI. Curley's wife

    A. Flirting with the workers

    B. Talking to Crooks, Candy, and Lennie in the barn

    C. Persuading Lennie to listen to her

VII. The hope and power when people have companions

    A. George and Lennie

    B. Candy

    C. Crooks

VIII. The misery of each when companionship is removed

    A. Crooks

    B. Candy

    C. George

Topic #2

The novel *Of Mice and Men* is written using the same structure as a drama, and meets many of the criteria for a tragedy. Examine the novel as a play. What conventions of drama does it already have? Does it fit the definition of a tragedy?

Outline

I. Thesis statement: *Steinbeck designed his novel* Of Mice and Men *as a drama, more specifically, a tragedy.*

II. The novel can be divided into three acts of two chapters (scenes)

    A. First act introduces characters and background

    B. Second act develops conflicts

    C. Third act brings resolution

III. Settings are simple for staging

IV. Most of the novel can be transferred into either dialogue or stage directions

    A. Each chapter opens with extensive detail to setting

    B. Characters are described primarily in physical terms

V. The novel fits the definition of tragedy

    A. The protagonist is an extraordinary person who meets with misery

    B. The story celebrates courage in the face of defeat

    C. The plot ends in an unhappy catastrophe that could not be avoided

Topic #3

There are many realistic and naturalistic details in Steinbeck's *Of Mice and Men*.

Discuss how Steinbeck is sympathetic and dispassionate about life through the presentation of realism and naturalism.

Outline

I. Thesis Statement: *Steinbeck displays a sympathetic and a dispassionate attitude toward man's and nature's condition through the use of realistic and naturalistic details.*

II. Realism—things as they are

    A. Setting of chapter one

        1. Water

        2. Animals

        3. Plants

        4. People

    B. Description of the bunk house

    C. Dialect and slang of the characters

    D. Dress and habits of the characters

    E. Death as a natural part of life

III. Naturalism—fate at work

    A. Animal imagery to describe people

        1. Lennie

        2. Curley's wife

    B. Lower class characters

    C. Place names

        1. Soledad

        2. Weed

    D. Foreshadowing

       1. Light and dark

       2. Dead mouse and pup

       3. Lennie's desire to leave the ranch

       4. Candy's crippled dog

       5. Solitaire card game

    E. Symbolism in the last chapter

       1. Heron and snake

       2. Gust of wind

       3. Slim's comment

Topic #4

The story of George and Lennie lends itself to issues found in the question: Am I my brother's keeper? Does man have an obligation to take care of his fellow man, and what is the price that must be paid if the answer is "yes" or if the answer is "no"?

Outline

I.   Thesis Statement: *Steinbeck shows that there is a great price to be paid for not being sensitive to the needs of others as well as for taking care of others.*

II. The vulnerable ones

    A. Lennie

    B. Candy

    C. Crooks

III. The heartless ones

    A. The boss

    B. Curley

    C. Curley's wife

IV.   The insensitive one—Carlson

V.   The sensitive ones

    A. Slim

    B. George

Topic #5

The American Dream is for every man to have a place of his own, to work and earn a position of respect, to become whatever his will and determination and hard work can make him. In *Of Mice and Men* the land becomes a talisman, a hope of better things. Discuss the American Dream as presented in the novel.

Outline

I.   Thesis Statement: *For the characters in this novel, the American Dream remains an unfulfilled dream.*

II.   The dream

    A. Owning a home

    B. Enjoying freedom to choose

        1. Activities

        2. Companions

    C. Living off the fat of the land

    D. Not having to work so hard

    E. Having security in old age or sickness

III. The dream's unrealistic aspects

    A. Too good to be true

      B. A pipe dream for bindle stiffs

      C. Lack of money

IV. George and Lennie's attitude toward the dream

      A. Was a comfort in time of trouble

      B. Did not really believe in the dream

V. Crooks's attitude toward the dream

      A. His belief

      B. His disappointment

VI. Candy's attitude toward the dream

      A. His belief

      B. His money

      C. His disappointment at the end

Bibliography

Fonterose, Joseph Eddy. *John Steinbeck: An Introduction and Interpretation.* New York: Holt, Rinehart, and Winston, 1963.

French, Warren G. *John Steinbeck.* New York: Twayne Publishers, 1961.

Marks, Lester Jay. *Thematic Design in the Novels of John Steinbeck.* Paris: Mouton, 1969.

McCarthy, Paul. *John Steinbeck.* New York: Frederick Ungar Publishing, 1980.

Steinbeck, John. *The Short Novels of John Steinbeck.* New York: The Viking Press, 1953.

Steinbeck, John. *Of Mice and Men.* New York: Bantam Books, 1988.

Available at your local bookstore or order directly from us by sending in coupon below.

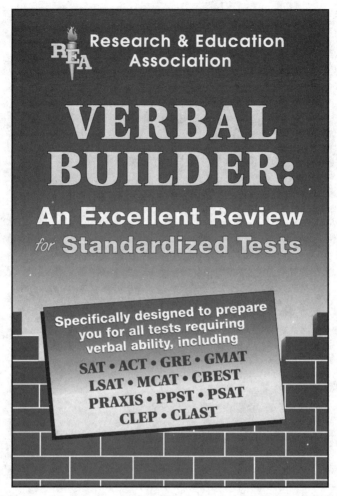

Available at your local bookstore or order directly from us by sending in coupon below.